AF270067

Written by Noah Leatherland

BASKETBALL

PowerKiDS press

Published in 2025
by The Rosen Publishing Group, Inc.
2544 Clinton Street, Buffalo, NY 14224

© 2024 BookLife Publishing Ltd.

Written by: Noah Leatherland
Edited by: E.C. Andrews
Designed by: Jasmine Pointer

Cataloging-in-Publication Data

Names: Leatherland, Noah, 1999-.
Title: Basketball / Noah Leatherland.
Description: Buffalo, NY : PowerKids Press, 2025. | Series: World of sports | Includes glossary and index.
Identifiers: ISBN 9781499448955 (pbk.) | ISBN 9781499448962 (library bound) | ISBN 9781499448979 (ebook)
Subjects: LCSH: Basketball--Juvenile literature.
Classification: LCC GV885.1 L384 2025 | DDC 796.323--dc23

Manufactured in the United States of America
CPSIA Compliance Information: Batch #CW25PK. For further information contact Rosen Publishing at 1-800-237-9932.

Find us on  

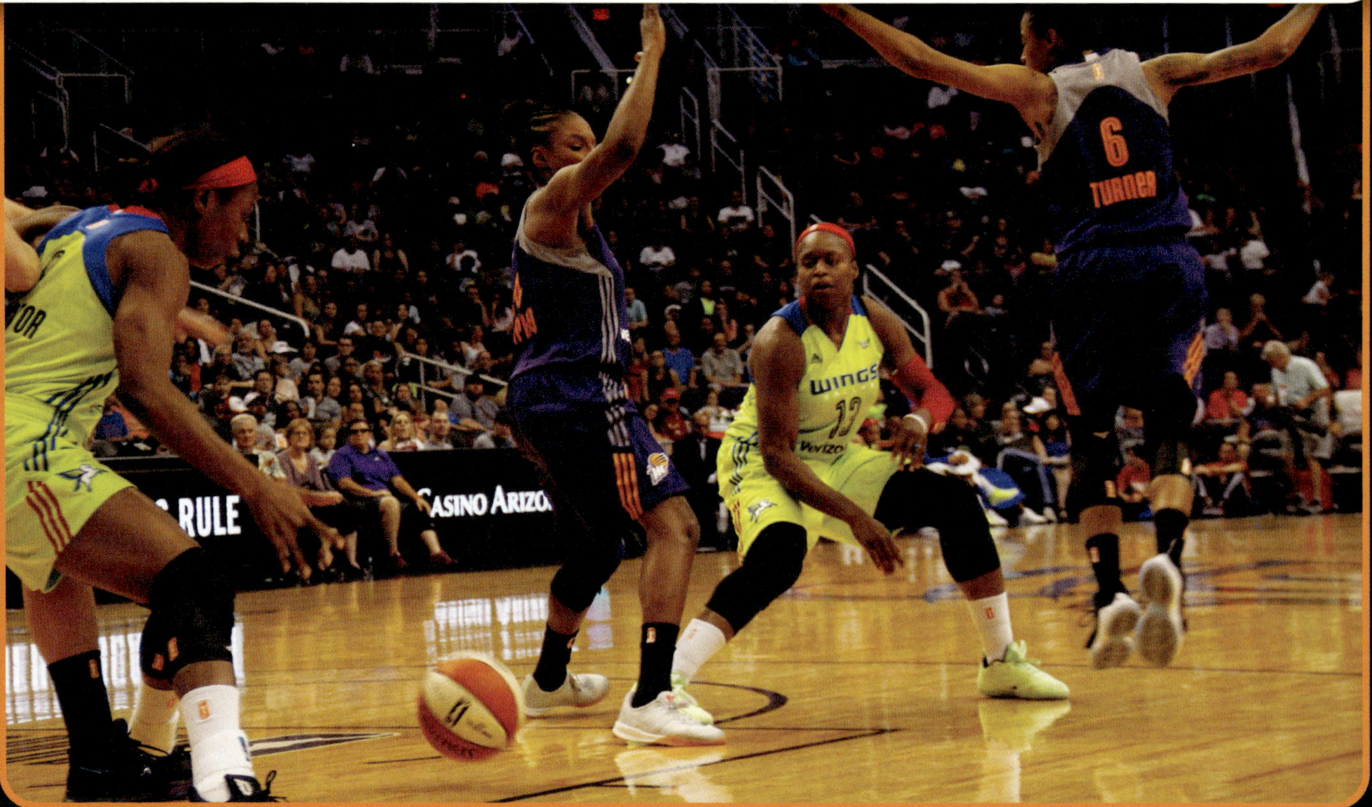

IMAGE CREDITS

CONTENTS

WORDS THAT LOOK LIKE THIS CAN BE FOUND IN THE GLOSSARY ON PAGE 24.

TIP-OFF

Playing sports can be a great way to spend time with your friends while also keeping your body healthy. Do you have a favorite sport?

Basketball is a fast, energetic game that can be really exciting to watch and play. Basketball games usually see both teams score lots of points. Basketball players work together to score points for their teams.

THE BASICS

A game of basketball is played by two teams of five players. Each team has a set of **substitute** players who can be swapped in. Teams can substitute players as many times as they need.

The aim of basketball is to throw the ball into your opponent's basket. A basket can be worth one, two, or three points. The number of points scored depends on where the ball is thrown from.

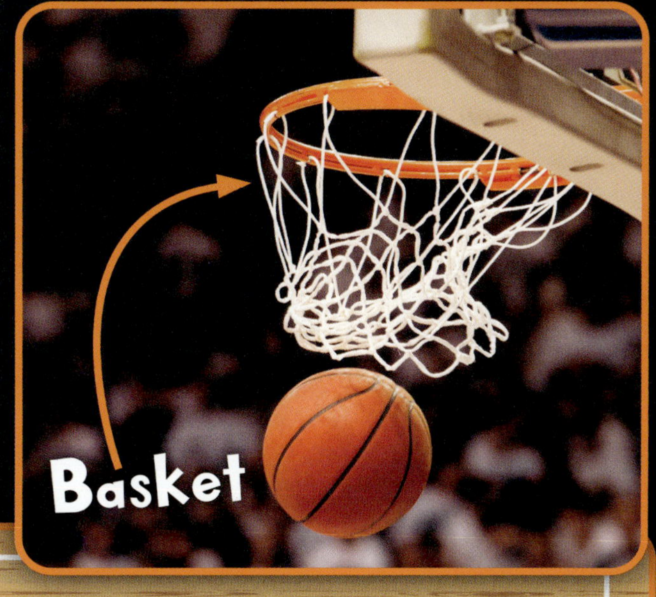

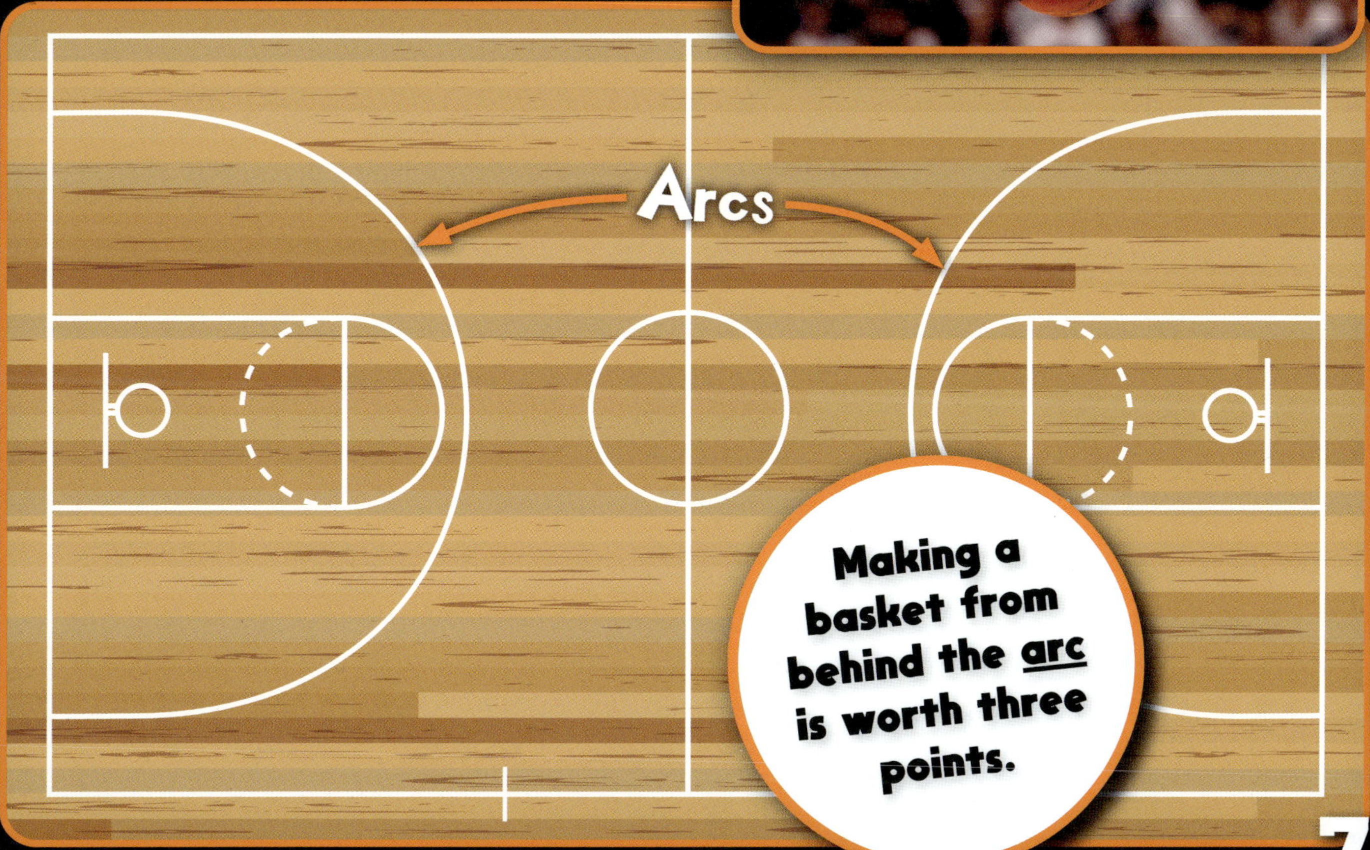

Making a basket from behind the arc is worth three points.

POSITIONS

Each team has five players on the court, and there are five different positions they may play. Each player has a different job to do depending on their position.

Point guards are usually the leaders of their teams. They are often the ones who drive the ball up the court toward the basket. This creates chances for their team to score.

A shooting guard's main job is to shoot the ball towards the basket. They are usually the best in their team at shooting from far out and scoring baskets worth three points.

Power Forward

Power forwards are strong players. If the ball bounces off the basket, it is called a rebound. A power forward's main job is to grab these rebounds and make sure their team still scores points.

Teams usually put their tallest players in the center position. Centers usually score points from close to the basket. Centers also use their height to help their team defend by blocking the opponent's shots.

A small forward is the most <u>versatile</u> player on a team. They move all over the court to help their teammates. They help to shoot and score from up close and from far out.

TACTICS

Different basketball teams use different <u>tactics</u>. Some teams like to move the ball up the court quickly. Others like to take their time and work on <u>plays</u> that they have created with their coaches.

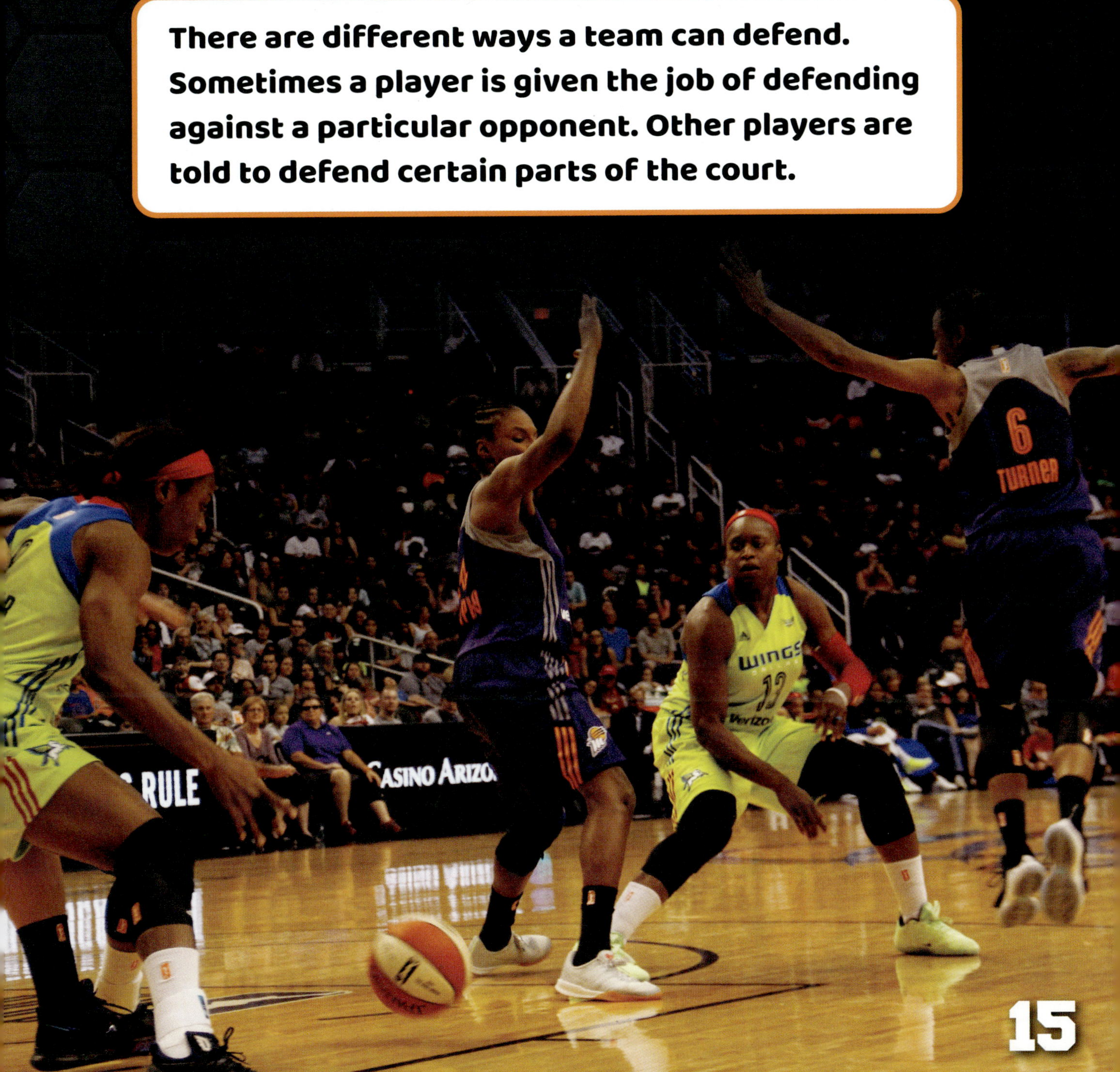
There are different ways a team can defend. Sometimes a player is given the job of defending against a particular opponent. Other players are told to defend certain parts of the court.

FOULS

Referees look out for players breaking the rules. Breaking a serious rule is called a foul. If a player gets too many fouls, they are not allowed to play the rest of the game.

When a player makes a foul, the other team is given a free throw. A free throw is a chance to shoot at the basket without the other team being able to stop them.

Free throws are worth one point each.

WATCH THE CLOCK!

Basketball players need to keep an eye on the shot clock. The shot clock is a timer. It tells the players how long they have to shoot once they gain <u>possession</u> of the ball.

If a team does not shoot by the time the shot clock runs out, the other team is given possession of the ball. The shot clock in the NBA is just 24 seconds long!
Some shot clocks are on the basket.

THE FINALS

The NBA and <u>WNBA</u> Finals are the biggest competitions in basketball. The top two teams in each league play against each other to decide who will be that year's champion.

Games in the NBA Finals draw huge crowds!

The two teams play each other in a <u>series</u> of games. Whoever wins the most games in the series is declared the winner.

Basketball is a game that is watched and played by millions of people all over the world. Basketball can be played anywhere. All you need is a ball and a hoop!

You could gather a few friends and play a game of basketball, or maybe you could join a team near you. Whoever you play with, make sure you keep practicing and have fun doing it!

GLOSSARY

arc	a curved line
NBA	National Basketball Association
opponent	the team one is playing against. Also, one player on the team being played against.
play	plan for how players will move and act
possession	when one team has control of the ball
series	a set number of games played between two teams
substitute	something that replaces something else
tactics	planned ways of doing something
versatile	able to do lots of different things
WNBA	Women's National Basketball Association

INDEX